Flying School

Robert Saxton was born in Nottingham in 1952. He lives in north London and is currently a freelance editor and writer. He is the author of six previous books of poetry: from Enitharmon, *The Promise Clinic* (1994); from Carcanet/OxfordPoets, *Manganese* (2003), *Local Honey* (2007) and *Hesiod's Calendar* (2010); from Shearsman, *The China Shop Pictures* (2012); and from Angle Shades Press, *Six-way Mirror* (2016). He is also represented in Faber's *Poetry Introduction 7* anthology. In 2001 he won the Keats-Shelley Memorial Association's poetry prize for 'The Nightingale Broadcasts'. See www.robertsaxton.co.uk for more information.

Robert Saxton

Flying School

Shearsman Books

First published in the United Kingdom in 2019 by
Shearsman Books
50 Westons Hill Drive
Emersons Green
BRISTOL
BS16 7DF

Shearsman Books Ltd Registered Office
30–31 St. James Place, Mangotsfield, Bristol BS16 9JB
(this address not for correspondence)

www.shearsman.com

ISBN 978-1-84861-642-4

CONTENTS

Inventions

Skylark

Air and Angels

The Secret Shire

in memory of my dear father,
Colin Saxton (1925–2017)

Inventions

The Chinese Wheelbarrow

The Coach and Horses

At the end of a long day's bone-
shaking journey you might just fall
from your carriage – as if some crazy
stowaway had spent the whole trip
pummelling you. All around: a mess
of broken veins, the old Roman roads.

No less broken are these *new* roads,
thrown together like a gristle and bone
broth for a dog or slave, a mess
made of a meal – worse than a fall,
a kick; instead of a business trip,
a forced march on useless crazy

wheels travellers pretend *aren't* crazy.
Starting a shared life on such roads
makes a young couple see their trip
as a perversion, bred in the bone,
of their walk up the aisle. They fall
out, bitterly – marooned in a mess.

Rain churns up an even worse mess:
lanes turn to lakes. One man's crazy
enough to race against nightfall,
slogging in boots down perilous roads
to the next inn, drenched to the bone.
Sickness feeds off a desperate trip.

Cart and wagon find any trip
arduous in the dark-age mess
barbarians brought, the backbone
of the land in countless crazy
pieces, paving stripped off old roads
for self-defence as ramparts fall.

Sooner than feed prices will fall
for horse and ox, angels on your trip
will wing you high above the roads
gratis, tidying the mortal mess!
Light-freighted beasts need a crazy
lot of hay, on roads dry as bone.

The fall of empire leaves a mess
of crazy centuries that trip
on a wishbone: throwaway roads.

The Chinese Wheelbarrow

Who in Europe knows that faraway
China manages roads better? Tracks,
narrow and paved, unscroll beside
rice fields, lakes – vast network
of peaceful, unambitious life,
winding like sheep's bowels. The wheel-

barrow, with one big central wheel,
more useful than a cart in every way,
even on cliff paths where a goat's life
looks precarious, on most tracks
makes little of the pusher's work:
the wheel takes the weight, each side

laden with goods, or on one side
a single traveller, the wheel
tilted to compensate – skilled work,
not arduous. Along the way,
larks fill the ear as if these tracks
were the precincts of the good life.

Laying them makes a peasant's life
pious and fruitful. On the side
of heaven are those whose tracks
move taxable wealth on a wheelbarrow, letting no double pathway
rob two flanking fields of work.

A village breathes out sounds of work,
shuffles and shouts of family life,
chickens running every which way.
Late morning brings around the side
of a house two feet and a wheel,
bearing a Venetian tired of tracks,

though appraising the web of tracks
he's travelled as a masterwork,
the perfect match for this strange wheelbarrow, everywhere ferrying life.
Some recruit the wind to their side.
A fleet of twelve a mile away

one day he spies, and tracks the life
of sideways sails putting wind to work,
heaven's way of helping a wheel.

Wandering Aengus

In the unpolluted Ireland of white moths,
those uncommercial samples of the stars,
a weary rag-and-bone man trotting home
with all those wretched tossed-out rags and pans
hears ribald tales drifting from shadowy bars.

He's heard them all before: the one about
the monk whose mistress was another monk
whose cowl and vow of silence kept them safe;
the one about the skeleton stalking souls
kicked out of pubs, penniless or blind drunk;

the one about a love-struck Englishman
in Limerick who spent a fool's fortune
on a clockwork egg that couldn't tell the time
for the Taoiseach's wife, for what? – worm-eaten
apples, the bollocks of a clapped-out moon.

Shakespeare & Co.

A new quirk in bookshops
is students swiping pages
until the penny drops:

they're in the dark ages,
with bookish fools or fops
wheezily turning pages.

Though in the modish camp,
you too may drag a book-
asaurus from the swamp,

not quite extinct. 'Geeks, look!
With that weird scholar's lamp
he's wormholing a book!'

On shores of card and glue
you part seas of paper
to lead your cravings through.

Truth vanishes like vapour,
all the sense you construe
lost on scraps of paper.

Parkour

Athletes of the *favelas* are meddlesome
children unleashed from the imperturbable womb.
Mean city streets are their gymnasium.

Elysian playground initiates defy the laws
of gravity, eagle-hearted players
gorging on the world by ripping back its layers –

dormers, plinths, aerials laying down the same
challenge as stinking sewers, the victory dream
proven true: these heroes are what they seem,

vaulting the senate house zoo of bullies and liars
on a penthouse trapeze in stolen running shoes,
without fear or parachute, nothing to lose,

tossing losers a lesson even they'll understand.
Everyone can jump. Not everyone can land.

Taking to the Air

'O, for a horse with wings!'
                    Cymbeline III ii

Though we swim in the sea
        without flippers or fins,
when we reach for the sky we're undone.

We stay stuck, like a tree,
        to the earth for our sins,
no more suited for flight than a stone.

You can flap like a bird
        while you bounce on your springs,
like a fool. This will only exhaust you.

You can follow the herd
        on an aeroplane's wings,
but that's cheating – besides, it will cost you.

Manoeuvring a kite
        as it floats on the wind
might bring you a sense of well-being.

But for bodily flight
        of the Superman kind
there's a method that's much more like skiing.

Forget all ideas
        of soaring up high:
go with gravity's downward subjection.

Fall and face your worst fears –
    you're unlikely to die
with a parachute's simple protection.

Falling feels more like flying
    when you gracefully pause,
like a bluebird a mile above Dover.

You'll believe you're defying
    known physical laws,
though you'll land with a bump when it's over.

The Sacrifice

Most packers are would-be jumpers,
so longing for a drop they sneak
the back way into the club house
like spies, mingling with the members.
You might see one in a small group,
chatting, winning over strangers
with an off-colour anecdote.

Catching his eye, you hold his gaze,
plumbing the dark well of his need.
You know already he'll agree
to the time-honoured covenant:
long hours of packing parachutes
for no reward but the slim chance
of a drop if someone cancels.

You watch him from the high walkway.
He weaves his hands in the entrails
to ensure the shroud lines play out
before the canopy, falling
separate, true and safe as rain
from its cloud, the shaman drawing
water from his own raging thirst.

Aerial Flowers

after Paul Nash, 1944

I

When suddenly war came to us, the sky
appeared to lower, as if on Doomsday,
hovering like some giant bird of prey,
malignant angel in the moment's eye.

Constantly we looked up, expecting terror
to fall. My instinct was to interrogate
the clouds, in fear, or else to penetrate
the deepest blue for weapons hidden there.

Also I scanned the vastness of the sky for
parachutes – what the Spanish describe
as 'roses of death', emblems of a warrior tribe.
They'd haunted me ever since the Spanish war,

a dreadful miracle I had to strain
my eyes to spot: white flowers, like poison rain.

II

Although my first war picture was a collage
of these self-same roses, the powers that be
preferred my vision of the soul set free
from the prison of its derelict ribcage

aloft inside a cockpit of white light,
exploring the habitations of the dead
to find, among circus wires, its aerial bed,
the cloud-draped refuge of eternal night.

I knew the Ministry officials would declare
my asthma made me unfit to fly. Even so,
they appointed me as war artist to show
illustrious victories in the blood-splashed air,

but only through my imagination's eye –
they signed up a factual recorder to testify.

III
What they expected I shall never know.
I drew and painted sixty chariots
of the air but not one airman rattling shots
at enemy planes. Eventually they let me go

in favour of a veteran comrade
famous from the last war who'd made it known
he wanted to paint heroes, our home-grown
harvest of courage defying the reaper's blade.

What intrigued *me* were the incongruous
impacts that tore the Luftwaffe apart,
littering the downs, consuming a farm cart,
scattering fragments all around a lighthouse,

strewing a nunnery with wreckage burnt to ashes,
orphaning pheasant chicks in cornfield crashes.

IV
I painted these daily disasters from the start,
for their intrinsic interest and their value
as propaganda – for our enemy, a cue
to despair; for us, a gladdening of the heart.

My employers didn't see things quite that way.
Even when my subject was planes in flight,
still they were displeased: something wasn't right
about my images, which went astray

in treating my theme unpatriotically,
emphasising the unique character,
or 'jizz', of each angelic monster,
dowsing for its genius empathically.

I was pleased to find echoes of my view
among the Air Force – both ground staff and crew.

V
By the time I left the Ministry I'd seen
that boneyard of broken planes near Cowley,
Oxfordshire – the astonishing Dead Sea,
with breakers of metal crashing on the plain

like a tide caught in a petrifying gaze.
On a moonlit night at times you'd almost swear
these body parts moved as they'd moved in the air
to chase the foe or dodge destruction's blaze.

In truth the only motion was a barn owl
on silent wings, predator over predators,
quartering the dump of death with twitching claws,
raking deep shadows, ruthless on the prowl.

Following this hunter on its ghost patrol,
I'd see it capsize to take a rat or vole.

VI

My first large pictures of this place were done
under the patronage of an advisory
committee of airmen who'd encouraged me.
My inner war, however, was far from won.

The kind of flight I wanted proved elusive.
Mind must achieve what body is denied.
Modern ways of flying were spiritual suicide –
not nourishing, not thrilling, not exclusive.

The misconception seemed to lie in making
flying apparatuses heavier than air –
gigantic, deafening contraptions where
overcrowding made things worse. Heartbreaking!

Vast, lonely space, and silence, were my needs.
These planes, moreover, flew at distressing speeds.

VII

And so I dreamed, most of the daylight hours,
hoping to find expression for the style
of flight I craved, listening and looking while
I strolled in my garden, picking leaves and flowers.

One twilit evening as I made my way
along a path, peering to pluck nightshade
blooms (so ethereal!), there came into my head
this eerily whispered communiqué:

'Last night heavy and medium hellebores
bombed the mountains of the Moon.' As I turned
back to the house, the ideas for which I'd yearned
came to me abundantly, like toadstool spores

adrift among my neural synapses,
making amends for recent creative lapses.

VIII
I gathered together all the elements
of a collage, inspired by the weird
oracular pronouncement I'd just heard,
with its aura of mystic intelligence.

First I chose Cattermole paper, the colour
of a moonlit night, to serve as my ground;
then dried and pressed hellebore flowers I'd found
in a dusty tome by some long-dead scholar;

and finally seed pods seemed exactly right
for bombs descending in their gentle rage.
On top of this I'd carefully need to gauge
what to draw or paint – a cloud? a meteorite?

I cut out a moon plate from my second-
best book of the skies: Nasmith. He wouldn't mind.

IX
The image failed – too hasty, I confess.
I nudged the moon, which made a flower cup slip,
falling like a parachute on the crater's lip.
Such misadventures couldn't have mattered less,

so long as I continued to explore
all possibilities of aerial imagery.
From dawn to dusk I scouted tirelessly,
like a samphire gatherer on a lonely shore,

or rather like those valiant engineers
who, ahead of the infantry, holding their breath,
probe for mines, feeling inch by inch for death –
the surrogates of all our mortal fears.

For death, I see now, was my subject – to die,
let's face it, being the only way to fly.

The Cosmonaut's Free Holiday

Vzmorye Holiday Centre, Estonia, 1970s

Lopsided Jupiter, low in the night
    above the trees,
belittles our mission like a socialite
sneering at peasants. Still not quite at ease
outside our helmets, earnestly we shake hands
with scientists who appear embarrassed
by our stumbling efforts to frame in words
a reverence none of them understands.
Our stirring impressions whirl like cosmic dust
or surplus grain put out to feed the birds.

If we're the heroes of the golden age,
    as all concur,
co-authors blazoned on the title page
of the book of the glorious future
of the Soviet Union, why on Earth
is this vacation venue so austere,
the gift of a spartan, empty box of planks,
no cupboards, no drawers, no plugs – a dearth
of utilities in a cabin built for fear-
ful interrogation, not a nation's thanks?

Or so it seems, and so I thought until
    it dawned on me:
clothes fallen from useless hooks into a pile
on the floor are reminders of gravity,
beloved comfort sorely missed in space.
Luxury would be dangerous so soon
after touchdown: we need to decompress.
Where better than this intermediate place

of deprivation? – somewhat like the moon
in its neighbourly unworldliness.

Our true rewards will follow. National Pride
        Day in Moscow,
the heroes in a Red Square parade glorified
with medals, band music, flags, a salvo
of confetti; then a swanky river cruise.
Compliments deflected with a humility
even Politburo chiefs can't but admire.
Later, Star City. Western jazz and blues.
A dacha with a bench beneath a tree
for daily sessions training to retire.

The first woman in space, Valentina
        Tereshkova,
unkissable in her helmet, keener
on rockets than men, smiles from her poster
facing me at breakfast with radiant love
for her country, balm for my sore eyes.
I didn't get a wink of sleep all night –
there were beech martens in the roof space above,
scratching, uttering infernal mating cries.
I fled my cabin, trudged the beach till first light.

And now they've changed my room – I made a fuss
        and then pulled rank.
The new one seems worse, though no doubt martenless.
The toilet flushes non-stop from a hidden tank;
the shower, lacking its rose, pours like a tap;
the window, high and small, won't open at all;
the underfloor heating's forever stuck on high;
the bed's constructed on a base of scrap;
there's lewd graffiti on the bathroom wall.
Winged patriots can make a nest in any sty.

Skylark

Farmyard Serenade

We settle in our crèche of lambs,
　　luxuriating in the whims
　　　　indulged by extra, freelance limbs.

Then, in the hay loft, hearts and hands
　　start playing like fox cubs, all our wounds
　　　　returned unopened to the hounds.

The Midnight Summons

after Propertius

Midnight – I ask you! What a time to receive
a letter from my mistress insisting I leave

right away and hasten to her in Tivoli!
I thought of those twin towers commanding me,

that hint of bliss embodied in bare white hills,
the Anio's waters tumbling to placid pools.

What should I do? Venture into the night
trusting its dark disguise to spare my throat

from an attacker's knife? If I disobeyed,
my fate would be worse than being waylaid

by some ruthless brigand. Displeasing her
brought me banishment once for a whole year,

with loss of her company, not just her bed.
She'd be quick to push me down among the dead.

*

Besides, lovers are holy, their wanderings charmed.
They can stroll among highwaymen unharmed.

To a lover who braves the Scythian wilderness
even barbarian nomads show largesse.

Moon and stars anoint us with their mystic gleam;
Cupid by torchlight guides us towards our dream.

Hostile guard dogs, catching a stranger's whiff
as he walks by a homestead, soon lay off

making their furious racket behind the fence:
they're hushed by love's disarming ambience.

Even in areas prone to opportunist crimes
we lovers may roam in safety at all times.

With such thin blood no felon would stain his shirt.
Venus herself shields locked-out souls from hurt.

*

And if this trip ends in quietus anyway,
that's a price, I know, I'll be content to pay.

She'll bring me perfumes and deck my headstone
with garlands, keeping vigil, in tears, alone.

May the gods forbid she'll lay my bones anywhere
too crowded, like next to a main thoroughfare

thronged with a vulgar, chattering multitude
stepping in dog poo and discarded food.

Such lovers' graves get desecrated, even
while raising their first flowery prayers to heaven.

So bury me in some lonely, leafy copse
or on a distant shore where no boat stops,

in a bar of sand where crabs and waders play.
I'd hate to be a name on the public highway.

October Hornpipe

On that St Luke's Day there was fine hunting
in the woods. Bright bugling pierced the autumn air,
clouds galloped on a wild chase of their own.
Having ridden for nearly two hours, King
John, needing to rest a while somewhere,
slowed to a trot and stopped by a mill, alone.

The miller's wife was the only one at home.
Flustered to have an uninvited guest
so impossibly grand, she proffered cider,
beer, game pie, fresh-baked scones, a honeycomb.
Ten minutes later the pair were half-undressed,
fervently kissing, when in walked the miller.

From the kitchen block the husband snatched a knife,
and stepping forward in a fog of rage
he shook it, readying himself to dice the spleens
of his whoreson king and harlot so-called wife.
That made His Majesty hurriedly engage
in bargaining for his soul by shameless means.

'What if I give you a title? Make you lord
of all the land from Charlton yonder to where
the river bends beyond Rotherhithe? What if
on this holy day of Luke I award
you the licence to hold a yearly fair
in the village? Agreed? Put down that knife.'

At first the venue chosen was a green
across the way from the parish church, Saint
Luke's. Later the Fair was moved, as if for shame

at how its character had turned obscene,
to the far edge of the village. Without restraint
pandemonium cavorted. Riffraff came.

In paintings the ox was St Luke's attribute,
recalling how his writings emphasise
Christ's sacrifice for our imperfect race.
Yet horns are also a badge of disrepute,
abundant at the Horn Fair in the guise
of mockery, where mercy has no place.

The cuckold's horns were the Fair's relentless theme.
Many wore or carried a pair. Stalls sold
horn knick-knacks – combs, snuff boxes, paperknives.
Each entrance arch had horns nailed to its beam.
Even the gingerbread men had little cuckold
's horns, discrediting their gingerbread wives.

Jokers of all ages enjoyed lifting
forefinger and thumb behind an unwitting head.
Revellers in droves indulged in the ribaldry
condemned by Defoe: the Devil soiling
the clean white linen of the Church's bed.
How deep the stain of pagan depravity!

A troupe of actors launched the day's
diversions, comically re-enacting the scene
of conjugal betrayal at the mill.
This set the tone. Cross-dressing, both ways,
sharpened the mischief. Jokes going round, unclean
to begin with, soon turned filthier still.

Next morning you might find bodies littering
the grass, like corpses on a battlefield
or a wolf's victims strewn in a sheepfold.

But these are just drunks asleep, dishonouring
in their dreams the bright angelic shield –
not horn but, so tradition tells us, gold.

Venetian Nights

Just before turning to her little Columbine
to confirm she was the comeliest and cleverest
the court could remember in a thousand years,
the Dogaressa offered me the heaped teaspoon
of a smile, of the kind that graciously
acknowledges ardour while gently reproaching
the foolishness that permits its expression.

She is, after all, Her Highness the Dogaressa
and me the emissary of a dreamlike kingdom
so many months of hazardous sailing distant,
with possibly a wife for each day of the week
(that is, if the tropic calendar *has* weeks)
and a habit of *connubio a tergo*, as her priest
might say, or some such savage aberration.

Yet in this rare slim volume pulled from her
library of smiles with exquisite arm and hand
reaching to the limits of decorous self-containment,
even a Polynesian could read of beguiling mysteries,
among them the Doge's rumoured schooling in love
by Casanova captive in the Leads, his sentence
shortened by a month for every hour's instruction.

For if these tales are true, no one can know but she
(or both if she is expressive in their intimacies)
what pleasure he gave at first, what progress he made,
his standing now, and whether she has entered yet
some heavenly sphere on any of his nighttime visits.
Her smile caressed such secrets, but for a moment
allowed me the treasonable thrill of speculation.

Ours

Clothes, like leaves, uncoupling, falling.
      A summer visitor grieves,
   with one or two others,
      prescient, still in love with you.
Keenly a kettle's boiling

but we're in bed already, telling
      each other we've all the time
   in the world for once.
      I'm like a baby, curled
in your qualities. Nothing's spoiling.

Consolation Prize

*'Dropping one's car keys in a grate is likeliest
in the vicinity of one's car.'*

Sky fills empty nights.
Now and then a wand,
since you're lonely,
flashes loss among sums
of stars, a private storm:
landfall no nearer.
Some relief this brings.

Some meteorites
contain diamond
clusters of only
twenty-five atoms,
small enough to form
the stones if bacteria
wore engagement rings.

Lacuna, Lacuna

We're kissing
in a light that truly flatters.
We're whispering sweet nothings all night long.
    What's missing
is the only thing that matters.
Will I say so? I don't think so. Is that wrong?

    We're trying
to mop the tears that fall when hearts break.
A new love heals and makes the lovelorn strong.
    We're buying
a jalopy for the parts' sake.
Will I say so? I don't think so. Is that wrong?

Constellation Street

Doors and Windows

A house with soulful windows,
    among them several bays,
        sleeps through its doom of days.

Challenged by dreamless doors,
    who'll break in, climb the stairs?
        Somebody's home. Nobody dares.

The Magic Horse

Each stone hoof grows wings.
    So: just blink. You'll start to woo …
        enchant … enthral.

It's one of those things
    you half-think you can half-do
        but can't … at all.

The Road Not Taken

Love adrift, cold now. I'll cope – touch wood!
Who wanted this? The answer is, both
of us … unless I misunderstood
the runes. I'd beam us back if I could
to when we talked about change and growth

that damp, dark day of the country fair.
Then I still had some power to claim,
to persuade – our cogs showed little wear.
I'd have taken you in my arms there
and then if I'd thought you felt the same.

You had a nest of kids. My path lay
elsewhere, a lone fight against the black
dog. Could I imagine you one day
pondering the road not taken? No way!
Bright souls look forward, dark ones look back.

The cost of friendship is every sigh
I've silenced. Our talk is upbeat. Hence
that sick feeling in the heart when I
leave you or put down the phone or by
some rare lapse let slip our difference.

Preset Image Valentine

Intimacy these days discomforts. More our style
is the park or the pub, or three-minded chess
with young Kasparov. A colon-dash-bracket smile
implies we have no longings to confess.

Always, though, I'll text a bunch of preset flowers
on the eve of her six-month scan. 'Thank you, dear
heart, for remembering.' Then come the hours
of worry (agony for her) before the all-clear.

Valentine's the patron saint of squirm for us both,
love's wafer on the tongue a poisoned biscuit.
The troubadour-lover worth his sugar composes

a romantic effusion of the kind she'd be loath
to wipe her *derrière* with. Dare I risk it?
I text her a preset pint pot, foaming with roses.

Skylark

High in the sky and in my head
    that long-lost, much-missed flight of song
replayed your tenderness in bed,

copious and vigorous above,
    hovering, teasing, sweet and long –
the gift and given of your love,

which like the skylark folded up
    within itself its own farewell,
so passionate that even hope

required no landing in its voice,
    before the shock of silence fell,
continuous, like we had no choice.

Overnight Guest

It's more helpful, I suppose, than a footprint:
a pair of 3D boots parked in the hall,
showing pleasing compliance with my carpet rule,
though troublingly alien. Gigantism
has a foothold: they're 11s for heaven's sakes!

Beside them, on the mat, there's more than a hint
of pathos – my innocent at risk, in thrall
to a cornpole cowboy? You were still at school
when I bought these 4s for your trek to wisdom.
Daughter, tread carefully. Watch for rattlesnakes!

Air and Angels

The Goldfinch

Carel Fabritius pinxit, 1654

Having blinked away my trust,
    she plots to win it back.
The mind's eye fills with mist.
    If we're pledged to honour the look
of things, what hope for our tryst
    now this error's caged in our book?

A coin in a miser's purse
    surrenders its gold wing-flash,
chained convict's caprice
    of arrows held in the mesh
of art – the frontispiece:
    enslaved imprisoning flesh.

The taxidermist's ensign
    is grotesque: imported bud
detained in quarantine,
    betrayed by a careless word.
The painting's thief has seen
    the 'yellow', *American* bird.

Air and Angels

Rabbits frolic, playing families. A squat
    Doric temple sits chalky-white and proud
on a furrowed hill, the only pilgrim
    a farmer on a tractor, his straw hat
squinting out from the prophetic cloud
    of ninety-nine gulls transfiguring him.

Badgers wrestle in a ditch. A fieldfare
    flock feasts on berries in a rowan tree
tingling with dew. And now, like an angel,
    precipitate in the autumnal air,
an idea forms, which helps good souls to see
    how angels might be more corporeal.

If the temple frieze has four sets of scenes
    sculpted upon its metopes (let's say,
the arts, religion, war and industry),
    common sense tells us of a human means
of contemplating this entire array
    of the state of England with godlike eye

from just one place: that is, to exhibit
    the four friezes round the walls of a room
in a gallery, turning them outside in
    to let the pilgrim view them inside out,
as if the Redeemer from His broken tomb
    had shown us how our gladness might begin –

how, over English fields and hedges, seven
    angels in woollies and pleated skirts, hair
nicely done, might fly with flasks of seeds,

tilting them to broadcast hopes of heaven,
red linings hidden like the humblest prayer,
the spiritual undersides of earthy tweeds.

The Silent Collection

after Stanley Spencer, The Dustman *or* The Lovers

Every day the dustman forgets himself
in cleansing labour, in his striped jersey,
brown corduroy trousers and black beret.
Every night he forgets himself in love.

He's not unhappy with his earthly lot:
it's just that he's ambitious for more bliss –
more life in every dustbin, every kiss,
a stronger infusion in the moment's pot.

Like love affecting everything we do,
home taken to a finer point of feeling
distils not downwards from a mystic ceiling
but outwards from the useful and the true.

Good things discarded years before their time
may still disclose their lustre through life's grime.

*

On collection day bystanders gather round
the dustman ecstatic in his wife's embrace,
her love for him so strong with erotic grace
she lifts him, like a child, right off the ground.

As if waiting their turn, the others watch
in two little clusters, male and female,
patient for their destiny to prevail,
the consummation of a spotless match.

Each loves the rest, in an atmosphere
of joy as peaceful as the privacy
of a lavatory. Such blessed intimacy!
Bored with hopscotch, the dustman's kids appear,

diving into bins for a fitting homage:
old teapot, empty tin, limp leaves of cabbage.

Sarah Tubb and the Heavenly Visitors

Stanley Spencer, at his easel

A comet can but shouldn't scare
like this one did. She knelt and prayed
at her gate. The heavens should thrill,
not inundate, the heart – restore,
not fell, unless the mess we've made
has stoked an avenging fireball.

That was dear Granny Tubb, long gone,
but since her face eludes me now,
that gate prompts me to think instead
of Sarah in her ma's black coat,
shawled, bonneted, broad of beam –
her body on loan from the dead.

I lived near her on the same street,
which in my childhood seemed merely
a long place where I'd apprehend
a dark recurrent entity –
the street was aligned east to west,
her house being at the sunset end.

My sexual consciousness contrives
to make such women seem strangely
more worshipful, now I could choose
to marry into their mysteries.
Sarah is pure meaning to me,
like a cherished doll with a soul.

Three thoughtful angels hear her plea.
The gifts they bring are things she loved:

a papier mâché homily,
a postcard rack one visitor
hands to my cousin Annie Slack
who keeps the village shop next door.

And standing here is our grocer,
pulling at one of his braces
and letting it go with a thwack
to wake himself out of heaven.
This painting is for such as him,
since today is the world to come.

At Cookham Regatta

There's one long side of rope and one of water.
Within the makeshift frame of the regatta

a temporary village teems. With untimely pride
I walk down the towpath aisle my next year's bride

towards an archipelago of singular souls
at play, around a fakir barefoot on hot coals,

a wild hog roast, a volley of foaming hoses
aimed at painted flames a clever machine opposes

to the village brigade's courageous action stations,
a charlatan touting humanist cremations.

There may be racing shells, a catamaran or two –
it's hard to tell for the throng that blocks our view,

among them clowns on stilts, flag dancers, acrobats
on a tower, ladies with swan and peacock hats.

Strolling towards the enclosure's shorter rope flank
but loath to pay for entry, we veer from the bank

diagonally inland across the yellowing meadow –
for parsimony we'd be voted best in show.

The infernal din of heavy metal's glory years
is in any case too much for our delicate ears.

Ten minutes later, the peace for which we yearn
conceivable again, pre-nuptial thoughts return.

We set our hearts on a pot of chamomile tea
in the teashop opposite the bridal atelier.

Suddenly she screams and in panic grabs my arm,
staring down in terror at some demonic harm

through a tear in the fabric of the world's soul
only she can see, being virtuous and whole:

an aid convoy bombed, with Red Cross workers dead;
a carer bludgeoning a grandmother in her bed.

All innocence disproved, all heavenly love defiled.
'It was a snake,' she cries, 'or a lizard, something wild.

'I saw it scuttling across the path in front of me
into the long grass. Horrible! Can we hurry

'on to the broader road ahead? Now, please!
I'm a city girl – I know you love to tease.'

This time I don't. Troubled by such squeamishness,
I silence the voice of reason nonetheless,

strangely aware of snakes along the track,
slithering out of sight as we hasten back.

Jimson Weed

after Georgia O'Keeffe

This flower, too small for you to see
in the time you have, means more to me.

And so I'll paint it big. Then the surprise
will rub away the hurry from your eyes.

*

This flower now means something to you
as well as me – still less, it's true,

and usually something you bring,
which invariably for me is missing.

World's End

Other Than What One Is

One couldn't really be anything
other than exactly what one is –
a tramp, a refugee, a king;
a Chen, a Salvador, a Liz.

Just imagine if one were, say,
Donald Trump by an accident
of birth, winning over black and gay
voters in the bid to be President;

or Melania, his beautiful wife –
jewellery and skincare entrepreneur,
philanthropist, sharp as a knife,
America's best depression cure.

The thing is, these good folk exist,
and if one could become one –
Don, Mel, anyone on one's wish list –
what would have changed under the sun?

Don would be Don, as he is now;
Mel would be Mel, with all her bling.
But they'd be also you somehow.
And the one you were would be nothing.

Zoo Party

A two-legs (male) gets trapped in a big cat's genes.
Taiwanese zips snarl, threatening in orange manes.
Hark at the howls of Tarzans and their Janes.

Nagel, you've got it wrong: a dog can learn
new tricks. Flap out of your bat cave and spy on
a bozo who knows what it's like to be a lion.

Vienna Consultation

'Let me check your pulse.'

'Buccaneering Keith Richards at a formal
dinner, tieless, winking at the marchioness.'

'Your heart rate is normal.'

'Lord Byron discovering an opera diva
undressing in his gondola cabin after his morning swim.'

'You have a slight fever.'

'Adam, pre-eminent father of the first nation,
intoxicated by the beauty of his clone-mate Eve.'

'Are you taking any medication?'

The intern transcribes verbatim into her notebook
the measured opinion of Dr Agnieszka Zorniak de la Tour:

*'Imagining one is somebody else during coitus,
less common than mentally substituting an alternative partner,
is usually related to issues of self-esteem.'*

'Pharaoh, let me tell you about your dream.'

The Golden Scarab

Carl Jung, in his poetry notebook

In her dream all is just
    what it seems: heart of dust,
with green-gold wings at rest,
    rich and cold, the soul guessed
from its case, drawn to tears,
    a dark place for stuffed years.

The tomb clock swings its cross,
    sells red rock as the moon's loss.
This bug chimes with *my* dream,
    of royal crimes in the steam
from a hot tub. Love flows
    where the rot takes the rose.

The Crossroads Tree

A flyer's impaled
    to advertise
the fluttering
    promise of careers
an ocean from
    these leaves and tears.

Improvident woodsmen
    set their course
for ship or barn
    or chest or hearse
oblivious of
    the crossroads curse.

They should have left
    the mast of news
intact in acres
    of lost trees
to raise the rooted
    from their knees.

The saw will now
    slice knots and gnarls,
a pilgrim's
    courage in its sails,
hell-bent on heaven,
    wrecked on nails.

Top Withens

A surgeon attending the ruin
          furnishes the faltering brain
with iron seals against the rain.

Yearning gaps are re-walled,
          roofless passion is re-tiled.
Staves are stacked against the wild.

Literature is mostly rust.
          The end of the pilgrim's quest
is neither shelter nor rest.

The Wink

At Lamorna Cove, Cornwall

On this lawless coast a cove,
like the bird trap of a grave,
a rock-strewn, roofless cave,

disgorges from a green lane
where painted on an inn sign
a smuggler's leering, malign

wink claims no one is moral.
We're most ourselves when we steal.
Only the grotesque is real.

Well-intentioned relic-bound
pilgrims are never too grand
to detour for contraband.

Nobody's called a poor wretch
whose treasure shines from a ditch.
Mud cakes the boots of the rich.

A brazen signal mirrors
the true self with giving gaze –
conjunction of blazing rays.

Knowing the lusty grave fills
so soon, we break the king's rules,
leaving citizenship to fools

too frail for storm-tossed singing,
sweetened by the ocean's tang.
We're proud death is in our gang.

Albatross

The Pilot

Flying ace
on his cross,

quick dark moth
in grey rain,

blood splashes,
bits of plane,

bright soul so
far from lost

a tall plinth
in red earth

awaits his
homecoming,

unharmed, dead
or wounded.

The Poet

Trench jacks face
battle stress,

drifting north,
chronic rain,

slipping toe-
hold on most

things fine (food,
luck, love), sane

hope all spent
of home's earth,

obsequies,
war's ending,

iambs instead
dismembered.

The Priest

Seed of grace
caught in dross,

spleen of wrath,
where shells rain

and the crow,
pagan host,

from its rood
drapes a stain

on the scent
of hale breath,

bends to kiss,
forgiving,

a forehead,
faith undead.

The Poppy Seller

Bugle trace,
endless loss,

grateful mouth
tasting rain,

black sashes
for the slain,

slush from snow,
keep each ghost,

each imprint
of each breath

warm for this
reckoning:

all bloodshed
remembered.

Revenant at a Wedding

Blind danger,
    never lifted
for all who loved
    the law,
at night came nearer
    by a crooked mile,
caring nothing
    for all we loved,
putting love itself
    on trial.

Kind stranger
    whom we gifted
my murdered
    father's heart
slow as a bearer
    walks me
up the aisle,
    with something
like my murdered
    father's smile.

Intrepid Retirement Journal

A bushbaby, close to me, weeping,
    seems unlikely to forgive.
Our friendship's not for keeping.
I've unsubscribed from the concubine's blog.
    Where are the nutrients I need to live?
I'm sightseeing in Beijing in the smog.

A chimp with shampoo, showering,
    is hardly a chimpanzee,
any more than a thought, flowering,
makes a garden of the brain.
    Trying to swing, I fall. I hurt my knee.
I'm trailblazing in Congo in the rain.

An errant fruit bat, wounded, grieving,
    distracts me from lost friends.
A room is loneliest when it's heaving.
Mirages campaign: 'Heal. Mingle.'
    Outside is where company ends.
I'm hiking to Serenity Point, in shingle.

Roxanne's *Jeu d'esprit*

Deep in the Neverglades
there's a crashed flying machine,
the local inventor's dream horse,
baroque in its ingenuities,
easily recognisable among
more ordinary airplanes lost
to civil war and family feuding
by anyone prepared to venture
this far from reach of map,
land radio and common sense.

One day into Les Mille Magots
walks Roxanne, sixteen,
apprenticed in the art of
bourbon drinking, seasoned
with a dry, gravelly humour,
making creditable progress in both.
After ordering, and taking a first
swig, on the bar she unwraps
a damp black sweatshirt to reveal
a mouldy pair of aviator goggles.

She shows us these *in situ*
in a photograph, not a great image
in the dim aquarium light
but the goggles just discernible
around the skull, the skeleton
cropped at the fourth pair of ribs.
Thoughtfully she acknowledges
her debt to the waterproof casing
Grandma Slothrop gave her genius
hilarious brother last Christmas.

It is, in fact, a fake (using
her brother's teaching skeleton,
which after failing medical school
he smashed in two in a rage,
and her father's Air Force kit
from Korea, salvaged from the attic),
a set-up in the Thensome estuary
at the bottom of their garden,
hidden from suspicious eyes
by vines cascading from cypresses.

I learn the truth of this a year
later from her brother, Quail,
sharing a campfire with him
in 'Nam beside our grounded
Huey. The tail rotor in pieces,
I struggled with the wild spin,
clearing thick trees to land
on the fringes of a cleansed village,
in a playground with charred swings,
shell craters, unthinkable detritus.

We talk in the night amid
jungle noises so loud we scarcely
hear the radio telling us help
is coming – though I have my doubts,
and am inclined to pray, not to God,
since I have lost my faith,
but to America, mother and father
of our destiny, in whose name
we are draining the black swamp
of the corrupted soul.

If I survive this mission,
and the war, I pledge myself

to a mission of my own,
to track down Roxanne in
Les Mille Magots, back in
the Neverglades, rescue her
from the clammy hands of
old Colonel Brainmash,
coax her playful spirit toward
the light and, like a rib torn

from a teaching skeleton
planted in the yearning soil
of a good man's admiration,
watch her slender form shimmer
into beauty in a gauzy
white dress at a party with
a hundred guests on the banks
of the Thensome river.
Hearing this, Quail smiles,
moments before I lose him.

The Inspection Cover

The serpent stands upright on its tail
    with the Imperial Inspection Cover
balanced on its head like a halo.
    It has risen, of course, from the sewer,
slimy, with the stink of the Congo.
    It is spouting undiluted nonsense –
something about the glide from vertical
    to cerebral, and envy being a stage
on a creature's path to transcendence,
    a leviathan outgrowing its narrow gauge.

Hooded like a monk, the cobra
    safeguards its wisdom, an elixir
in a phial in a tragedy – useful
    when, still in shock, you climb the stair
to a spare bedroom, vertical
    with horizontal this first lonely night,
the former outranked by the latter.
    Once you stood face to face, feet to feet,
then sat somewhere, speaking of flight
    and tunnelling, which would one day meet.

The Signature

We all found hurt and hope in everything.
There was an ibis wrapped in oblivion
in an attic. A hard-boiled private eye
was recruited, working with the expert.
Along one toe was a fabled signature,
a window into a world of shadow,

nimble torchlight frisking deeper shadow
in which a teardrop sparkled like a thing
of beauty in a museum, its signature
a pulse of ownership prior to oblivion.
Tight letters betrayed neurosis to the expert
in handwriting with her cold eagle eye,

a *femme fatale*. Here prowled the private eye,
struck by her Nefertiti eye shadow.
Since in pharaonic ways he was no expert,
maybe she'd condescend to teach him something –
heartache as proof against oblivion,
along with the secret of that signature.

Each devil and deity leaves his signature
as token consideration to the eye
lifting a dripping memory from oblivion.
Love throws on life its little black shadow,
dressing to kill and breaking everything
breakable just to upset the expert.

Bronze feathers, mentally light, aren't expert
enough to corroborate the signature –
yet another blind alley. Everything

appears disposable to the X-ray eye,
stands in a line-up without a shadow,
shivering, and stripped for oblivion.

In the plot they pitched against oblivion,
the forger, the private eye, the expert
staked various futures on the same shadow,
fooling each other with a passable signature,
too fleeting for the skull-embedded eye,
racing leftwards, fading into nothing.

In the waiting room of oblivion nothing
we want outstays the shadow's signature
flushed from rare angles by an expert eye.

Faith and Truth

A dialogue in the marketplace

Bambini of the liberal élite,
you hate the tiniest imperfections. Spoiled?
You've never mourned a disappearing street,
run for your lives or in a desert toiled
to break up stones with stones to make ends meet.
At your hearth no slumbering venomous snake lies coiled –
only a dog deflea'ed, its collar coned,
or a cat whose rodent gifts are not condoned.

This binary view is preposterous at best.
Even Wall Street has its losers' share of pain.
The bonanza of the meritocratic West
sees many an arrow skewer its wagon train.
Then there's disease: the cuckoo in the nest
of paradise. The worried well in vain
insure each organ, synapse, follicle, joint.
You're talking tosh. In any case, what's your point?

My point is faith. When life's a pit of vipers
we reach to the skies for an existential hug.
God speaks to us through loss – He'll hardly Skype us.
When you're really down to the wire you won't just shrug.
If the village well is targeted by snipers
you'll grab yourself a lucky water jug.
You'll find the faith denied to idiots tweeting
the bliss of using their phone to control their heating.

Hang on, my friend! It seems like what you're saying
is truth dawns when we sink down to our nadir.
When human effort fails we're left with praying.

The ego, self-sufficient in Arcadia,
elsewhere is fragile: faith prevents it fraying.
But isn't a vital principle betrayed here?
A worldview rooted deep in human weakness
has false perceptions, twisted by obliqueness.

Such logic is familiar though defective.
You think that truth is truly the preserve
of the Western university collective,
that long tradition from which scholars swerve
at their peril. Affinities are elective
but woe betide the fool who kinks the curve.
Nobody thinks straight when they're in distress?
The truth is, truth disdains a smart address.

A placebo God may lead you by the arm
to your final moment, quietly reassuring.
No looking back unmasks His specious charm.
The truth is comfortless as well as boring,
an abstract frame that stages our alarm.
Better to think of ageing as exploring,
content at last while others work the farm,
the plough unearthing fragments of belief
shined by the friction of a planet's grief.

The Tlaloc Supremacy

'President Trump listens to boots on the ground':
Afghanistan, August 2017

Rain trembles in its bowl,
hands upturned until
a child's still-beating heart,
aloft, disarms the threat
of drought – impotent springs,
enfeebled battle songs.

The first drop is a tear
on the steps of the tower,
one seed amidst our ruin
craving attentive rain,
all eyes upon the moat,
adopted umpteenth state,
starting to fill with faith,
blood, fear, decency, life.

*

The point of a leader's life
is to make his own faith
the conscience of the state,
encircled by a moat
replenished by social rain
from a stormcloud of ruin.

We honour from our towers
that nameless orphan tear,
immortal in our songs,
revived like native springs.
Our tribute is a threat

brash in the selfless heart
as fierce as war until
peace comes with its begging bowl.

Heavengate

A dialogue of light and dark

Our eyes, wide open like a gate,
    deny the spirit's crime.
Our banners flutter high and proud
    for penitents who crawl.
The self's the only real estate:
    the golden paradigm.

The happy harvest mustn't wait,
    we plough in earthly time.
While cowards kneel and cry out loud,
    the winners take the haul
of bullion that humps the shroud.
    You losers watch it fall.

A crown of lightning in a cloud
    of love redeems us all.

*

Your moaning makes no sense at all.
    You've looked down at the cloud
you were floating on: you were bound to fall.
    You've woven your own shroud.
It's this way to the heavenly hall –
    no naysayers allowed.

The break-out moment takes its time
    but never stops to wait.
The airship's punctured paradigm
    is all of your estate.

The chosen hate to see you crawl,
 so destitute and proud.

This muddle consecrates a crime,
 its headline 'Heavengate'.

World's End

I fuel the flesh, I launch the bone.
Frost on the runway glistens white.
The spirit grounds me like a stone.

The north wind howls its monotone,
the final call for the final flight.
I fuel the flesh, I launch the bone.

The nights are long, the days are done,
the hours crammed in their locker, tight.
The spirit grounds me like a stone.

Memories shed witnesses. Alone
I chart their course, in flickering light.
I fuel the flesh, I launch the bone.

My longings brighten those long gone,
like rescue flares in the savage night.
The spirit grounds me like a stone.

Darkness blinds, like something shone.
Storm clouds beckon, lightning-bright.
I fuel the flesh, I launch the bone.
The spirit grounds me like a stone.

The Meeting of Land and Sky

It doesn't matter how much life you sleep
so long as when you wake you learn to fly.
No one can have a grip on all those sheep.

The clouds are clinging and the hillside steep.
You scale the heavens with your weather eye.
It doesn't matter how much life you sleep.

The plane, omniscient, soars above the jeep.
You trace your yearnings on a country sky.
No one can have a grip on all those sheep.

The parachute subsides in a gentle heap,
saving its breath for freedom's battle cry.
It doesn't matter how much life you sleep.

In the long slow stumble to the lover's leap
late starters still find saviours to defy.
No one can have a grip on all those sheep.

The chasm plunges, doubtfully dark and deep.
Persisting leaves no time to wonder why.
It doesn't matter how much life you sleep.
No one can have a grip on all those sheep.

Frithelstockstone

for Jenny

At your house I imagine
numerous ley lines might cross,
re-vintaging your wine,
re-chlorophylling your moss.

Here you fought fierce cold
with brave words I was proud
to shepherd to their fold,
knit one purl one out loud,

warming but never woolly,
a heartfelt knitting pattern
unsheeply madly truly
itself, like wheat on Saturn.

No one will feel alone
who pulls your healing sword
out of Frithelstockstone,
where the grail of truth is stored.

The Immortality Show

Concentric circles of exhibits please.
Here leaves in a lunar wind rejoin their trees.

Here lovers, soft and sweet again, revise
their promises, pre-empting all those lies

that feed on what it seems they might have said
a purgatory ago, too wishfully, in bed.

Here reborn souls undream, undrink, unharm
themselves, repealing the flattening storm.

You'll wander round with wonder in your eyes,
happy at what you see: nobody dies,

or spoils a life because they're just too young
to know how not to or, alas, too wrong

in middle age, as errors proliferate.
Visit soon: some days they stay open late.

Valedictions

J'ay perdu ma tourterelle

The turtle dove, with chessboard wings,
purred from its damp, green emirate.
It sang its songs, it shined its rings.

We called a conference of kings,
each with his linguist to translate
the turtle dove, with chessboard wings.

Ten royal harpists swept their strings
to coax the turtle dove to mate.
It sang its songs, it shined its rings.

In sweet and simple outpourings
it wove a scarf of love and fate,
the turtle dove, with chessboard wings,

to ornament our shortcomings
so pointedly. Too long, too late
it sang its songs, it shined its rings.

With all the strength our weakness brings
we hammered to a five-bar gate
the turtle dove, with shredded wings.
We sold its songs and pawned its rings.

The Tree Cartoon

*'Who can impress the forest, bid the tree
Unfix his earthbound root? Sweet bodements! Good!'*
                                        Macbeth IV i

The tree cartoon, neither nature nor nurture,
has blagged its way onto the syllabus
of our top universities, where diehards view
this rogue subject as a pestilential weed –
a meme, if you will, in the wrong head-space.

Trees are surrogates for our vulnerabilities.
You can have a one-to-one relationship
with a tree. You can inflict more harm
than people usually bear. A philosopher
looks into your eyes, daring you to imagine.

If pain is the residue when goodness
is vacuumed off the planet, of course there *is*
pain – a clenching of the global organism.
Hence the *ouch!* when a tree unplants itself,
roots at full stretch snapping back like whips

to flail its own bark, and the consequent
convulsion of the canopy, a shiver
of self-correction. Then off runs the tree
to the blanket bog, where the whole performance
starts again. Yes, Flow Country is earmarked

for trees, but not this comical, hapless oak.
Foresters have more serious things in mind:
unwavering seas of lodgepole pine, Sitka spruce,
Douglas fir, black as the winter night,
livid with fish, twitching at exhausted stars.

In Wainwright's Footsteps

Close-cropped uplands, proud of their sinuous shape,
all beauty banked in joy of soar and sweep,
lull us to bedtime with superfluous sheep.

No one needs flowers so close to a lover's leap.
No plants grow tall. No wolves slink. Only sheep,
supreme, never lonely, graze on life's luscious lap –
though now and then one might fall from a lip.

We've put to flight our wishful post-war dream.
No longer, on fells, in dales, does nature teem:
wildness retreats within its human frame
while we, not noticing, ourselves turn tame.

Then, over all, the canopy of stars
sedates our conscience, purifies our prayers.
We spill more species each time we climb the stairs.

The Poacher Who Came to Our School

A teacher brought a poacher in one day
        to talk to our class.
More than one parent had been heard to say
we town kids lived inside a tower of glass.
We didn't even understand that cheese
comes from milk, bacon from pigs, trout from special
underwater farms. Would a poacher's expertise
on rural matters really be that useful
to us? Well, yes, according to our teacher –
though the urge to shock was his defining feature.

So there in his tatty old camouflaged coat
        a hobbit stood
by the teacher's desk, fondling a tame stoat
in his arms. All about his livelihood
we learned; how he slipped rabbits and eels to the poor
to mitigate the greed of the estate;
how at Christmas, as if in the Great War,
he and the gamekeeper fixed a football date,
each playing with his two sons to form a team.
The trophy was a brace of freshwater bream.

Two decades later, working in the City,
        I met the old Squire
himself – we sat on the board of the same charity.
'That poacher, helping to fight a moorland fire,
perished,' he said, 'after many terrible years.
We pulled his way of life from beneath his feet.
Subsidised to farm for wealth, we pioneers
laid waste to trees, hedgerows, flowers. The élite
got richer; the nature we cared for shrank.
With nowhere to hide any more, the poacher drank.

'I tracked him down once. His wife referred me
        to The Green Man,'
the Squire went on. 'Slumped in a sunken settee,
he listened to my own tales of woe – my plan
was to cheer him up by showing another side
of farming life. The interminable red tape!
Computer spreadsheets that make you goggle-eyed.
The view from the folly of glaring yellow rape.
We swapped our sob stories all afternoon.
Losing a poacher is like losing the moon.'

The Chicken of Tomorrow

Red jungle fowl, fighting in dirt till dawn,
    blood like rain sprayed in below-knee showers,
from spurs strapped on as natural as combs,
    wound and kill – with involuntary instruments
of their and their spectators' sacred will.

The ordinary American chicken hails from these.
    Our roosters crowed the American way,
though hens were prized only for eggs (the meat
    was scrawny in the war, when pork and beef
were set aside for troops, and chickens poor).

Humbly we eat. The weathervane rooster swings
    above our prayers for victory, decent despatch
of sons to duty, danger, far beyond the altar.
    Our diet is sorrow and, with selective breeding,
the great fat hen: the Chicken of Tomorrow.

In later years a drove of Japanese, parachuting
    from a high-speed bus in Louisville, Kentucky,
scurries through rain to the shrine. They have eaten en route.
    Around the Colonel's grave they place bonnets
of fried chicken, nectar-filled flowers for the brave.

The Secret Shire

The Big Zero

Although this landmark looms,
  darkening innocent whims,
unlambing sheepish limbs

while wolves above the track,
  clothed in the clouds, run thick
and hungry, there's a trick,

a spring, for the nimble heel,
  to know lost movement still
in the view from a high hill.

*

No gravid atmosphere
  drops ash upon the shire.
You blaze in heartfelt fire.

A sly, self-seeding smile
  proves change impossible
to keep, however small.

Love in the wintry groin
  pays rent in mist and rain.
Colours fill the shadows' grain.

*

Occasions step outside
  the flow, as if a word
were wielded like a sword

swung wild to fell the grove,
　　ripe moment's enclave
opened up like a grave.

Undaunted thrives the flower
　　even here, a well-hung door
a knife-blade above the floor.

*

A shadow in loud saloons
　　extends the day's returns
the inner child unlearns.

You spin time like a hoop,
　　the circular scope
of love, infilled with hope,

annihilating the dawn
　　and dusk of your own sun,
shining strong, never done.

Absences

I call at seven a.m.: the answerphone.
This always worries me, but it can take
quite a few rings to jangle him awake –
meanwhile I'm in the adrenaline zone.

It's easier when, one week in every four,
I stay with him in Notts, getting up early
to greet him with a pot of hot, strong tea
in the kitchen, first peeping round his door

to either, if he's conscious, say hello
or just observe the rising, falling duvet –
the reassurance of an ordinary day.
Then, squeezing past the stairlift, down I go.

*

It's different on this October morning.
He's in hospital, I'm strangely alone
in the house. I'll call him on his mobile phone
at nine. At seven I lie in bed, wondering

what I might do before my one o'clock
visit. Bird walk? Coffee at the Abbey?
Then as the heating cranks up fitfully,
something I hear delivers quite a shock:

a noise I thought was his but couldn't be.
These coughs I've always taken to be proof
of life must be the pipework in the roof,
floor or walls, breathing laboriously!

They're uncannily like him, as if a ghost
(merely on trial, I hope), keen to assert
verisimilitude, has chosen to alert
a guest to the reluctant absence of his host.

The Driving Test

What a pity there's no dual control –
and very little *self*-control, I know!
I'm shouting 'Dad, you've got to drop your speed!'
between rows of parked cars up the Woodhouse.
OK, the limit is thirty miles per hour –
but twenty might save the life of a child.

I'm like a parent with a wayward child,
understanding that my levers of control
are less effective than I'd like. An hour
of this is more than the gods could know
of mortal risk. Admittedly, the house
is hazardous too. But here it's unconscious speed

that's scary – that plus the opposite of speed
in his reactions. He's safer than that child,
painlessly mobile (not like in the house),
and demonstrating something like control,
but hesitant, moving in little fits – you know,
like a learner driver stuttering through their hour.

Actually, we're out for only *half* an hour –
enough to see his Achilles heel is speed.
He insists on his seven decades of know-
how, he's a veteran, driving to him is child'
s play. 'But even an expert can't control
his luck,' I say, as we pull up at the house.

There's a weird atmosphere in the house,
like an unpersuaded jury in the hour
of acquittal. After lunch I cede control

again, heading back south (at a sensible speed),
morphing from worried adult to lost child,
loosening myself from all I need to know.

No answer from the house just now. I know
I must control my morning panic's speed.
He needs another hour, like a sleeping child.

Wild Flower Refuge

By mid-October decent flowers
are few. Among time-blasted towers
of umbellifers and daisies,
ignored by the infrequent bees,
occasional specimens are found,
brave colours on the battleground
but all a touch embarrassed now,
perhaps at limping on somehow

amidst such devastation. Dad's
in the car, dozing fitfully. Fads
like my late-life botany bemuse
him, though he'll no doubt greet the news
of any findings I attest
as if he shared my interest.
His harvest's merely what I bring,
like spices gifted by a king

to someone helpless in the straw,
his crib the wheelchair or the car –
islands of peace, like long-sought flowers
I gather for our book of hours.
My photographs of what I've seen
enlighten less: the sun-bleached screen
showing petals, sepals, leaves and bracts
looks misted, as if by cataracts.

The macro lens is his, on loan
to me indefinitely, since soon,
in any case, it will be mine,
he says – he wants to reassign

the thing today. But I resist
this painful emblematic twist.
There's strength and time, a little yet
of each, and little to regret.

The Secret Shire

Portland Park and Bentinck Banks, Nottinghamshire, October 2017

As a child I wandered everywhere but here,
this jigsaw of woods, meadows and railway
banks – no one guessed the trains would disappear,
with the colliery they served. Instead we'd play
in the Misk Hills and the Warren, both freer
of adult contamination – that's to say,
foul mutterings from the black mask of coal,
the clank and grime that saved men from the dole.

Fifty years on, craving some solitude
and a country walk without a wheelchair
to push, the Quarries, I thought, might match my mood –
though I'd prefer a setting not so bare,
perhaps with wildflower meadows and a wood,
distractingly picturesque. I found these there,
amazingly! A stream in a broad tree-
filled ditch, the Erewash, slithered sluggishly;

and there *was* a meadow – shorn, flowerless –
but first, on my walk, a so-called 'bistro',
the Fat Rabbit, where I sat on the terrace
exchanging with dog walkers a brisk hello,
their dogs indifferent. The perfect place
for browsing my flower guide with a cappuccino,
tepid, but never mind – that was down to
me not doing a test sip at the counter.

Continuing, I came to a railway, this one
in use, it seemed – just: the Amnesia Line,
rails dull as scrap. Across the tracks was a zone

where flowers drank the dregs of autumn sunshine,
exiled in nature reserved for me alone,
a sanctuary clothing the skeleton of the mine:
devil's-bit scabious, campions white and red,
umbellifers quick amidst the standing dead.

It takes my dad all morning to get dressed,
which meant I'd several hours to explore
this time-warped Eden. Soon I felt refreshed,
anxiety for struggles behind his bedroom door
muted to background conscience by the quest
for species not yet seen, although I saw
enough to search more diligently here
next time, later in the shortening year.

Eidolon

Lips to his upturned forehead –
    chapel-chilled.
Unsettled memory
    suddenly defiled
by a fox shrieking
    like a demon child.

The window's view is just
    black night outside,
plus me, my thoughts at nine
    inclined to bed,
a useful trunk for
    everything unsaid.

Bereaved, I have myself
    become a ghost,
equally turning away
    from awkward guest
and, making matters worse,
    attentive host.

New Year in Provence

In memory of my father

In winter there are tourists but not many.
The Pont du Gard is lovely in golden light,
its arches ours alone, the river quiet.
I have new friends I'll never see again,
from whom in truth I'm longing to escape.
Alone feels best for the maladaptive heart.

I excavate his summer's happiest heart-
strained moments, not enough however many,
in the car or wheelchair, both an escape
from painful immobility, avenue of light
dappled with dread I'll never trace again,
even as a passive parent, loved and quiet.

Each day has too few interludes of quiet.
As breakfast and dinner threaten, the heart
takes stock for a precious hour, then again
from nine till bedtime, leaving me many
empty moments, neither heavy nor light,
to fill with birds and birders to escape.

But now it's them I'm eager to escape,
back to familiar solitude, the quiet
unchallenging disbelief, tinting all light
I move by, anywhere, even in the heart
of action here in Provence, so many
stories, places and listed birds. Again,

hundreds of cranes flock over trees. Again,
a wallcreeper has no elsewhere to escape

to. Black redstarts perch on masonry, many
approachable. Yet other birds too quiet
to see, or absent, both taken to heart
as loss, withhold from us their living light.

I recall the feather of his breath, so light,
then gone altogether, wafted again
to oblivion, drowned in the deep heart
of love, his only option to escape,
totally shut-down, enigmatically quiet,
with no thoughts at all, within my many.

By northern light I must travel many
roads with a hopeful heart, not to escape,
but find again some way to bless this quiet.

The Wallington Quails

A copy of the Imari originals, complete with box
but lacking the explanatory leaflet

These birds embellished Dad's bay window shelf.
Deflecting the suggestion my second cousin,
much removed, in mourning for her half-sister,
might cherish them, I earmarked them for myself.

Gifts most to the giver's taste come back again
with the unthinkable – fate being a karmic jester.
Each of the pair is a lidded pot the size
of a fist, white plumage splattered with black;

above the red bill, a tentative red crest.
They look like ptarmigans starting their disguise,
retreating with the moult of breeding finery back
to wintry white, soon to be totally lost

to predatory eyes in fold upon fold of snow
on the Cairngorms' vast phantasmal meadow.

The Casket

The desert enthrones its nomad in a box,
remembered on a trestle in my tent:
a snow dome sooty at the equinox,
a temporary thing so soon made permanent.

The gravity of loss pulls in my friend,
our tensions now and then discharged in hugs.
She comes to share my simple meal of sand
and helps to coax convulsions into shrugs.

Escape needs time, not motion, to succeed.
Grief sits here, licensed, garrulous, bespoke.
What makes the casket heavy: ash or oak?

More scattering is the one thing I don't need.
No ceremonial closure lets me choose
to tip him upside down, loosen six screws.

The Scattering

The idea took off, then rapidly lost height
and crashed in the flooded meadow of my grief:
to scatter my father's ashes at our barn owl site
while the owl was showing, like his phantom self.

There would be others there, and why impose
upon their thrill at catching airborne grace
a rite of closure for someone no one knows,
a fall to earth from so far out in space?

Briefly just now among the trees it flew.
Back home his ashes in their box sit tight,
a distillation soft yet scarcely light.

Tracking the owl, I know the last thing we'll do
together is the letting go of all I miss.
It can't be soon, although it must be this.

End Piece

after Rilke

Death is gigantic.
His muttering is all our mouths,
    all of us laughing, kissing, talking.
When we think ourselves most alive,
    he has the nerve
    to mingle with our breaths,
    weeping amidst our walking.

Acknowledgements

Thanks are due to the *The Spectator* (and to Hugo Williams, its poetry editor) for publishing some of these poems initially.

'Aerial Flowers' is in large part a rendering into sonnets of an essay by Paul Nash with the same title, though it omits Nash's opening pages and imports some material from other writings by Nash, especially on the subject of his painting *Totes Meer* (Dead Sea).

'Air and Angels' and 'The Silent Collection' have been published in *Stanley Spencer Poems: An Anthology* (Two Rivers Press, May 2017). The last stanza of 'Air and Angels' describes, with slight embellishment, Stanley Spencer's painting *Angels of the Apocalypse*.

'The Midnight Summons' attempts to be faithful to Propertius, *Elegies* III xvi, but with a few added details.

'October Hornpipe' borrows from a passage on the Charlton Horn Fair in Steve Roud, *The English Year: A Month-by-month Guide to the Nation's Customs and Festivals, from May Day to Mischief Night* (Penguin, January 2008).

'Intrepid Retirement Journal' was longlisted in the 2015 National Poetry Competition.

'Frithelstockstone' is dedicated to Jennifer Wilkin Shaw, author of *A Testament of Grief: One Mother's Story of Loss and Survival* (Simone Bluestock Publishing, April 2017).

'End Piece' was written in response to an approach by Charlotte Collins. Thanks are due to Charlotte for helping me understand some of the nuances of Rilke's German.

Many thanks to Gabriella Le Grazie for kindly taking the cover photograph for this book and allowing me to reproduce it: copyright in the image resides with her.

I'm immensely grateful as always to Peggy Vance for her invaluable support both moral and creative.

Lightning Source UK Ltd.
Milton Keynes UK
UKHW012018120319
338987UK00001B/29/P